To:

From:

Date:

Cheering You On:

50 Reasons Why Anything Is Possible with God

Holley Gerth

DaySpring

LIVE YOUR FAITH

Cheering You On: 50 Reasons Why Anything Is Possible with God
Copyright © 2020 by Holley Gerth
First Edition, March 2020

Published by:

21154 Highway 16 East
Siloam Springs, AR 72761
dayspring.com

Unless otherwise noted, all Scripture quotations are taken from the Christian Standard
Bible®, Copyright © 2017 by Holman Bible Publishers. Used by permission. Christian
Standard Bible® and CSB® are federally registered trademarks of Holman Bible
Publishers.

Scripture quotations marked NLT are taken from the Holy Bible, New Living Translation,
copyright © 1996, 2004, 2007 by Tyndale House Foundation. Used by permission of
Tyndale House Publishers, Inc., Carol Stream, Illinois 60188. All rights reserved.

Written by: Holley Gerth
Designed by: Heather Steck
Printed in China
Prime: J2095
ISBN: 978-1-64454-654-3

Contents

Introduction

At some point, all of us will face a challenge, have a dream, feel a little tired, fight a battle, or take a new step. In each of those situations, we need someone to give us courage, support, truth, grace, and hope.

The words on these pages will cheer you on in your journey. They'll help you keep moving forward in God's plan. They'll remind you He's relentlessly for you and nothing is impossible for you today.

Life is full of obstacles and transitions, goals and victories, setbacks and reasons to celebrate. God is with us in each of those moments. Nothing is too small for Him to notice, and nothing is too big for Him to handle.

Take these words to heart. Share them with the people you love. Go into whatever God has next for you knowing you are always loved and never alone.

Jesus said, "All things are possible with God" (Mark 10:27).

—Holley

You Have *Hope* and a Future

"For I know the plans I have for you,"
says the LORD.
"They are plans for good...
to give you a future and a hope."

JEREMIAH 29:11 NLT

God, You are our Creator and the One who knows every detail of our lives. You tell us that You have a plan for us. You promise to be with us always. You say You'll give us everything we need. We choose to trust You with our past, present, and future. Amen.

God chose for you to be here at this moment. He's watching over your life with love. He's sending others to encourage you. Even now, He's working out His good plan for your life. What's ahead for you will not be a surprise to Him.

On the days when life is hard, He will give you strength.

In the times that are happy, He will rejoice with you.

Even in the middle of what seems ordinary, He will do extraordinary things.

The hairs on your head are all numbered. The cares in your heart are all known. You will never be alone. If it ever feels like that isn't true, come back to these words and let them remind you.

God's heart and character will never change. Nothing can separate you from His love. He is always with you and for you.

Your past is full of grace. Your future is full of hope. Your day is full of possibilities.

God Gives *Holy* Confidence

"My grace is sufficient for you, for my power is perfected in weakness." Therefore, I will most gladly boast all the more about my weaknesses, so that Christ's power may reside in me.

II CORINTHIANS 12:9

God, this world tries to tell us that we need to have it all together. But what we really need to know is that You are the One who holds all things together. You give us more than self-esteem; You give us holy confidence. We are enough because You are enough in us. Amen.

What I've been realizing lately is this: the world tells us we need to have self-esteem, but what we really need is holy confidence.

For years I tried to prove I was enough. Perfect enough. Good enough. Experienced enough. Smart enough. Pretty enough. But it's only when we come to the place where we can finally say, "I'm enough not because of who I am but because of Jesus who lives in and through me" that our hearts get free.

The reality is, we are imperfect humans. But it doesn't matter, because our gracious Savior declares we are beloved and chosen and empowered *anyway*.

Self-esteem says we can do it.

Holy confidence says, in spite of us, God will.

In the moments when I'm insecure and afraid, when my heart is pounding and my knees are knocking, that's the truth I really need to know.

Maybe, just maybe, I'm not the only one.

There's So Much *Ahead* for You

Let us run with endurance
the race that lies before us,
keeping our eyes on Jesus,
the source and perfecter of our faith.

HEBREWS 12:1–2

*God, You are the One who frees us from fear and invites
us to run toward all You have for us. Give me the courage
today to take the next step and continue the race of this life
with endurance. I trust that You will provide
the strength and help I need. Amen.*

Fear often chases me. But today I pray, "Jesus, help me. I want to be free." Then a simple declaration comes to my heart: *I am done running away.* From now on, I am running toward.

I put on my tennis shoes when I get home. I walk out through the doorway and onto the trail behind our house. I turn on my favorite music and run like my life depends on it. *No more, no more, no more,* I say with every step.

I think of all I have run away from...how fear has chased me and people-pleasing has set my pace, how anxiety has nipped at my heels like a rogue chihuahua, how the lies have worn me out. *I am done.*

I will no longer be a woman who's defined by what she's running from.

I am going to run toward grace. I am going to run toward love. I am going to run toward the wild dreams that beckon me in the distance. I am going to run toward boldness and freedom and holy confidence. I am going to run toward Jesus.

I finish, sweaty and spent on the outside, strong and roaring on the inside. I don't know everything this new perspective means, what exactly I have done. But it feels like something dark and destructive challenged me to a race today.

And I won.

Strong, Brave, Loved

If God calls you to it, He will walk you through it.

—JENNIFER DUKES LEE

Fear *Can't Win*

Do not fear, for I am with you; do not be afraid,
for I am your God. I will strengthen you;
I will help you; I will hold on to you
with My righteous right hand.

ISAIAH 41:10

*God, You have compassion for us when we are afraid,
and yet You also give us courage beyond what we could
ever have on our own. You make us brave and fill us with
everything we need to accomplish Your purposes.
Fear can't hold us back. We are moving forward
with You. Amen.*

When God says, "Don't be afraid," it's almost always spoken to or for someone who is *already* afraid.

Israelite armies about to go into battle (Deuteronomy 20:1–4).

Mary being startled by an unexpected angel (Luke 1:30).

The apostle Paul facing a serious storm (Acts 27:23–26).

In other words, when God says "Don't be afraid," it is most often offered as a reassurance, not issued as a command. He's not saying, "Don't ever feel fear." He's saying, "Here's why you don't have to *stay* afraid."

"Do not fear, for I am with you" (Isaiah 41:10).

"Do not fear, I will help you" (Isaiah 41:13).

"Do not fear...I have called you by your name; you are Mine" (Isaiah 43:1).

It's the kind of language a parent would use to comfort a child who's afraid of the dark. A compassionate mom or dad knows their little one is going to be okay, but they give words that soothe hearts and calm minds anyway. That's the kind of love God offers us today.

God Will Come Through for You

> But I trust in You, LORD;
> I say, "You are my God."
>
> PSALM 31:14

God, we face challenges in this life. Even so,
we trust that You will give us the strength we need
to overcome whatever comes our way. We will not give
in to doubt. We will not let discouragement win.
We will not be defeated. Amen.

As Priscilla Shirer says in her book, *One in a Million: Journey to Your Promised Land*, the Israelites battled fear and insecurities. She says, "If there's a single word that doomed this generation of God's people from experiencing Promised-Land living in their lifetime, it's this one: 'nevertheless.' "

They had heard God's voice, seen His hand, and experienced His deliverance. Nevertheless they struggled to believe, trust, and obey.

I asked God, "What do I say instead of 'nevertheless'?"

And like shooting stars, two words blazed across my mind: *Even so.*

Yes, the situation is difficult. Even so, God will strengthen me.

Yes, I left my comfort zone and I'm afraid. Even so, God will use me.

Yes, it feels like the wilderness is endless. Even so, God will get me to the Promised Land.

Those two little words don't deny the difficulties or paste on a smile that says, "Everything is fine." They acknowledge life is hard. They recognize the obstacles. But in the end, they shift our gaze from what we see to Who we know. And that changes everything, especially us.

You're Already Amazing

Most People Don't, but You Do

For we are His workmanship,
created in Christ Jesus for good works,
which God prepared ahead of time for us to do.

EPHESIANS 2:10

God, You have made each of us unique and in Your image.
When we feel different than those around us, help us
remember that it's because we are. We're intentionally
unlike anyone who has come before us or anyone who will
come after. We give all of who we are to You. Amen.

Most people don't do what you do, love what you love, or feel the kind of passion you feel about a particular thing. This can make us feel like something is wrong with us. But I started thinking about this recently, and I realized we're in pretty good company if we feel like we're not like most people. After all:

Most people don't . . . build an ark.

Most people don't . . . lead people through the desert to the Promised Land.

Most people don't . . . die on a cross to save the world.

But aren't we glad one person did each of these things? If most people don't do what you do and you're passionately pursuing Jesus with your life, then it's probably not just a human plan. The heartbeat of God is probably somewhere within it. We need you, just you, to fulfill that purpose, complete that project, bring that gift to the world in a way no one else can.

Most people don't . . . but you do.

You're Already Amazing

God has
so much more
for us

than we can possibly imagine.

–JAIME SCHREINER

God Will Provide

He took the five loaves and the two fish, and looking up to heaven, He blessed them. He broke the loaves and gave them to the disciples, and the disciples gave them to the crowds. Everyone ate and was satisfied.

MATTHEW 14:19–20

God, You know all our needs and how to provide for them. You are limitless. You never run out of time, energy, or goodness. Thank You that we can trust You to give us more than what we want and that You instead give us what's truly and eternally best. Amen.

I'd never really noticed a verse that follows the five-loaves-and-two-fish story: "When Jesus realized that they were about to come and take Him by force to make Him king, He withdrew again to the mountain by Himself" (John 6:15).

Let's pause and take this in: Jesus had the chance to be the most popular person in Israel. But becoming a fish-and-loaves factory wasn't why Jesus was sent. He had His eyes fixed on the cross, the tomb, and eternal life with us.

Jesus didn't do everything others wanted; He simply did what God asked. No more, no less. He understood that while people thought another free meal would fill them, what they really needed was a Savior who could satisfy their soul hunger.

We will have requests to do many *good* things, but we can ask, "What's God's *very best* in my life today?" We discover the answer by spending time in His presence with His Word and by listening to His heart. Our loving God not only supplies but also multiplies. He will give us everything we need to do His will.

You Can *Lean* on Jesus

Come to Me, all of you who are weary
and burdened, and I will give you rest.

MATTHEW 11:28

*God, it's so easy to wear ourselves out by trying hard
and striving to be perfect. But all You ask of us is
to come to You and believe. You release us from
the burden of living like it all depends on us and
invite us to lean on You instead. Help us to receive
that gift of grace today. Amen.*

"Lord," I whispered, "I don't understand why I'm so worn out if I'm doing what You want. What lie am I believing?" In that moment it felt as if the Holy Spirit shined a flashlight on my heart and I could finally see this sinister sentence hiding in a dark corner: *It all depends on me.*

It all depends on me to make people like me.

It all depends on me to get the work done.

It all depends on me to be a "good Christian."

If that's true then "try harder" is the only reasonable response. But I serve the scandalously gracious Savior who said, "Come to Me." So I paused and asked Him, "What's the truth my heart needs to be set free?" And suddenly I realized: it doesn't all depend on me. *I only need to depend on Jesus.*

I forgot my role is obedience; God's job is results. Believing is all that's asked of us today. "This is the work of God—that you believe in the One He has sent" (John 6:29).

Jesus didn't die on the cross and come back to life so we could try hard.

He did it so we could live loved.

God Is *Your Source*

Be renewed as you learn to know
your Creator and become like Him.

COLOSSIANS 3:10 NLT

God, this world tries to tell us it's all about us,
but we want our lives to be all about You.
We want to reflect You in all that we say and do.
Help us to show Your heart, Your love,
and Your hope wherever we are today. Amen.

You are important to God's work in this generation. He has entrusted you with something very meaningful—a piece of His heart reflected in yours. You are made in the image of God, and there is a part of who He is that will only get expressed through who you are.

None of us can possibly contain all of who He is—only Jesus could do that—but who you are reveals a tiny bit of who He is in a way no one else ever will.

You may not feel qualified. You may not feel ready. You may not think you can do what He asks. Listen: you are all you need to be to do all He's called you to do. "It's not about you" can be hard words to hear, but in this context they can also bring a profound sense of relief.

You do not have to be Superwoman to make God's plans happen in your life. Because it's ultimately about Him, and your role is simply to let His light flow through you. You're the vessel—He's the Source.

You're Made for a God-Sized Dream

The size of our faith
isn't what makes
the mountain move.

The size of our God is.

—LEIGH SAIN

You Can Begin Again

Love covers a multitude of sins.

I PETER 4:8

God, You offer us Your grace. You show us Your mercy.
You encourage us to not give up but to simply try again.
You turn our messes into something beautiful for You.
Give us the courage to trust that we can always
begin again. Amen.

I take my seat and eye the blank canvas in front of me with suspicion. I'm here for a guided painting party with friends, and we laugh nervously as we consider the task before us. Then the woman next to me says, "The good news is, you can paint over any canvas."

Her words keep repeating in my mind and echoing in my heart: *"You can paint over any canvas."* They help me see the reassurance offered in Scripture from a new perspective. First Peter 4:8 tells us, "Love covers a multitude of sins." In other words, love can paint over any canvas.

Yes, even the choice we made that feels like it could never be forgiven.

Yes, even the secret that sometimes wakes us up in the middle of the night.

Yes, even the mistake that accuses us from the quiet, dark corner of our hearts.

The enemy of our souls would like to tell us, "You don't get a second chance." But the Savior says, "I died to give you as many chances as you need."

Art isn't about perfection; it's about the courage to try. Life is too. Every day is a blank canvas. So let's grab our brushes, dip deep into grace, and begin...*again.*

No One Can Take *Your Place*

We who are many are one body in Christ.

ROMANS 12:5

God, when we're tempted to think we need to be more like everyone else, help us remember that we only need to be more like Jesus. Help us to appreciate the differences You've created in each of us and understand how we reflect who You are more completely together. Amen.

I tentatively smile at the women surrounding the table. We've gathered to study God's Word, and yet beneath my calm expression I feel a twinge of anxiety. What if I don't fit in?

My fears are confirmed as those around me begin to share and I realize we're different in many ways. With a sinking feeling I think, *These are not my people.* Then, just as quickly, it seems God whispers to my heart, *But they are My people. And that's what matters.*

God created the body of Christ to be full of differences. It's His beautiful plan for us to need, help, and serve each other. What if, when we discover we're the only one like us, it doesn't mean we don't belong? What if it just means we've found where we're needed most?

I decided to stick with the group of women who seemed so unlike me. Over the next few weeks, we learned from each other and grew together. To my surprise, I discovered because we weren't the same, *I* wasn't the same by the end of our time together either.

In Jesus, it's our differences that can really make the difference. You have something to contribute. You are needed. Be who God made you to be.

Praise Is *Powerful*

Let everything that breathes praise the LORD. Hallelujah!

PSALM 150:6

God, we praise You for who You are and all You have done for us. We praise You when life is hard. We praise You when life is happy. We praise You in all that's in between. You alone deserve to receive glory. Amen.

The verse at the side is the final one in Psalms. It seems fitting that the close to this beloved book of the Bible is a simple phrase: praise the Lord. It's the one phrase we can always go back to, no matter what.

When we are tired, praise the Lord. When we're not sure what's going to happen, praise the Lord. When we're celebrating, praise the Lord.

Is this easy? Nope. Not in this world. Perhaps that's why the writer of Hebrews calls it "a sacrifice of praise" (Hebrews 13:15). Choosing to see God's goodness in all the moments of our lives does feel like a sacrifice at times.

And yet it's actually a gift God wants to offer us. He doesn't need our praise. Hard days can make us forget who God is and who we are. Praise reminds us. It brings us home to the place where our hearts can heal and find joy. It replaces the lies we hear with the truth we need. It lifts our hands and helps us lay down our burdens.

Let's praise God together. On the happy days. On the hard days. Today. Tomorrow. Forever. Amen!

What Your Heart Needs for the Hard Days

Focusing on God's provision
even in the smallest things
turns our minds to

thankfulness and praise.

—ANN SWINDELL

God Offers His Best

He lets me lie down in green pastures;
He leads me beside quiet waters.
He renews my life.

PSALM 23:2–3

God, in a world that pressures us to always be busy,
You offer us a different way of living.
Help us to say "yes" to Your best for us and let go
of the rest. You take such good care of us as we slow down
and allow You to do so. Amen.

I'll confess—there have been many times when "no" would have been the wisest answer to an opportunity, but instead I said a stubborn, exhausted "yes." And those choices took a toll on my soul.

So I can relate to these words God spoke in Isaiah, "You will be delivered by returning and resting; your strength will lie in quiet confidence. But you are not willing" (30:15). Lord, make us willing! Make *me* willing.

God has invited you not into more "busy" but into His very best. He wants to replace our hectic pace with heart-deep peace. He desires to free us from fear and give us true security. May we have the courage to slow down, let go, and live in grace.

We do not have to prove our worth by living "busy." We only need to remember we are already beloved.

Worry Can Turn to *Worship*

Don't worry about anything.

PHILIPPIANS 4:6

*God, it's so easy to worry about everything in our lives,
from little details to big concerns. That's so much
for our hearts to bear. Thank You for telling us we can
give all of our worries to You. You will carry them;
You will care for us. Amen.*

There's one activity in which I'm fairly sure I'm at the Olympic level. I am a world-class worrier.

I'm learning while my capacity for worry might seem impressive, it's actually oppressive. It wears me out. It steals my strength. It distracts my focus from more important priorities. It's simply not God's best for me—or for any of us.

Philippians 4:6 says, "Don't worry about anything." No exceptions or disclaimers. When I first read those words, I thought, "That seems impossible." Thankfully the apostle Paul goes on to give us a plan and a promise. He says, "But in everything, through prayer and petition with thanksgiving, present your requests to God. And the peace of God, which surpasses all understanding, will guard your hearts and minds in Christ Jesus" (4:6–7).

I don't have to let worry continue to wear me out. Even if I have weak moments, I'm going to keep building a new kind of strength through thanks and praise.

God Will *Guide* You

I am convinced that nothing can ever separate us from God's love. Neither death nor life, neither angels nor demons, neither our fears for today nor our worries about tomorrow—not even the powers of hell can separate us from God's love.

ROMANS 8:38 NLT

God, when we don't know what's ahead, it's an opportunity to remember who You are and how You've promised to always take care of us. Thank You that the future is in Your hands and we are too. Amen.

We all struggle with worry at some point. Every single one of us. It doesn't mean that God is mad at you or you're a failure. It simply means it's time to make some changes. And we don't have to make those changes on our own.

Jesus said the job of the Holy Spirit is to "guide you into all truth" (John 16:13 NLT). I love the word *guide* because it's an ongoing process rather than a one-time occurrence. As long as we are in this fallen world, we will uncover lies and the Holy Spirit will help us replace them with truth.

I also want to clarify that not worrying doesn't mean we don't think about the future or that we aren't concerned. We are to *wonder* about the future. That means considering what may be ahead so we can plan wisely.

If you're not sure whether what you're doing is worry or wonder, then pause and ask this: "Am I thinking from a place of fear or a place of faith?" Our part is fighting that fear and consistently choosing to focus on what God says instead.

You're Going to Be Okay

*When tempted to worry
about what might be,
focus on what is, was,
and forever will be—*

God's faithfulness to walk by your side.

—RENEE SWOPE

Light Is *Stronger* than Darkness

You are the light of the world.

MATTHEW 5:14

*God, when this world seems dark, we can trust
that Your light in us is more powerful than anything else.
You have called us to shine for You wherever we are today.
Help us to spread hope, share joy, and fill this world
with the light of Your never-ending love. Amen.*

The news drifts in from the other room as I sit at my desk and try to write. Heartbreaking headlines. Scary statistics. Pessimistic predictions. Feeling overwhelmed and helpless, I silently ask, "Lord, what do You want me to do about all this?" And it seems I hear a quiet whisper within my heart: *The only way to get rid of darkness is to add more light.*

As much as we'd like to, we can't go after darkness directly. We can only crowd it out with something better and brighter. Jesus lives within us and wants to shine through us. We don't need to have it all together. Sometimes it's through our cracks that the line shines through the brightest.

Our Savior knows there will always be news headlines like the ones I heard. But He also knows that because of what He did on the cross and through His resurrection, the darkness has already been defeated. And we can all make this world a little brighter wherever we are today.

Nothing Is Wasted

We know that all things work together
for the good of those who love God,
who are called according to His purpose.

ROMANS 8:28

God, You waste nothing in our lives. You take every bit of
what we go through—what's hard, happy, and everything
in between—and use it to make something unexpectedly
beautiful and of great worth. Give us eyes that see
from Your perspective today. Amen.

My mother-in-law stretches a newly finished quilt across the bed. "It's fantastic!" I tell her as I run my fingers along the careful stitching. She brushes off my compliment. "Oh, it's just a bunch of scraps put together."

As I consider this, I also think of how my life can sometimes look to me like a pile of scraps. I often don't see the possibility of beauty or usefulness in it. I see small. I see ordinary. I see leftover or left out. But in that moment I suddenly realize God doesn't share this perspective. The Maker of the universe, the One who is so big we can't even fathom His beginning or end, dares to endow our little scraps with the divine. He is the sewer of our stories.

This is the truth every tattered heart needs: There are no scraps in the hands of the God, the One who works all things together for our good (Romans 8:28). Every little piece will one day have a place and a purpose.

Nothing in our lives is wasted.

Bit by bit, God is making something beautiful out of all of it—and all of us.

God Is *With You*

The LORD will protect your coming
and going both now and forever.

PSALM 121:8

God, You are with us in every moment of our lives.
We are never out of Your sight, never beyond Your care,
always in Your presence. Thank You that even though we
don't know what may happen, we can be certain of
who will get us through whatever comes next. Amen.

God sees every detail of our lives. He's been with us in every step we've ever taken. This reassures me. None of us knows what's ahead. There are certain to be blessings and moments of happiness. There will also be hard days and tears shed. Some parts of our lives will stay the same and others, like it or not, will inevitably change.

Whatever may transpire, God will watch over it all. Every coming and going. Every beginning and end. Every dream come true and every heartbreak. He has done this for all of history. He is doing so today. He will continue to do so every day of this new year. Yes, every day of our whole lives.

We may not know what is ahead of us, but we can be absolutely certain of Who is with us. We are not random passengers, nameless and unknown in the crowd of humanity. We are beloved children of the God who breathed life into our lungs and who numbers every hair on our heads. Let's go forward boldly with the confidence that all things are possible and, in the end, all will be well.

God has already walked the road before us,

and He will walk it with us

today anew.

–COURTNEY ELLIS

Your Brokenness Is *Beautiful*

**The sacrifice pleasing to God
is a broken spirit.
You will not despise a broken
and humbled heart, God.**

PSALM 51:17

*God, You are not afraid of our brokenness.
What we try to hide, You often use to show Your glory.
We give You all the parts of who we are, every crack,
every imperfect place in our story. Make Yourself known
through us. Amen.*

There's an old story about two pots. One was perfect in every way. The other had cracks and broken places. Each day a woman filled the pots with rainwater she collected and then carried them down the path to her home. The first pot felt proud that she never leaked a single drop. The other felt ashamed, because no matter how hard she tried, she spilled a lot along the way.

One day the two pots overheard the woman talking with someone who lived nearby. The neighbor exclaimed, "The flowers along your path are so beautiful! What's your secret?" The woman answered, "One of my pots is broken, and the water that spills out helps the flowers grow every day."

If you're sitting there wondering if God can use you, then know that your greatest hurt will probably be your greatest ministry. We're all like the second pot in the story. God sees purpose in our brokenness even when we don't, and He can use it to bring forth beauty that blesses those around us.

You're Loved No Matter What

Love Is Powerful

Love the Lord your God with all your heart,
with all your soul, and with all your mind.
This is the greatest and most important command.
The second is like it: Love your neighbor
as yourself. All the Law and the Prophets
depend on these two commands.

MATTHEW 22:37–40

*God, You tell us that what matters most is love, not law.
This sets our hearts free. Help us to remember we're not
made for rules but relationship, not expectations but
acceptance, not demands but deep grace. Thank You for
reminding us what matters most. Amen.*

Someone once asked Jesus what mattered most, and He answered with the words in Matthew 22:37–40. As I read this passage recently I was struck in a new way by the sentence "All the Law and the Prophets depend on these two commands." Another way of saying it might be this: when we love, we have done everything worth doing.

This is a relief. It's a gift. It's the shredder we can put all the expectations and demands through until they are tiny pieces of confetti. It means the items on our to-do list are not a series of performances but opportunities to serve. They're not about completing but connecting. These are not pass/fail endeavors but heart-to-heart encounters.

I think the response of Jesus to the question asked of Him is about more than morality; it's about setting our hearts free. We are prone to strive and please and live like being on this earth is a job. We were not made for this kind of pressure. We were created, instead, to simply love and be loved.

Your Cares Matter

Give all your worries and cares to God,
for He cares about you.

I PETER 5:7 NLT

God, sometimes we think what we want most is control.
But what we really want even more is for someone to take
care of us. Thank You that we can give You all that weighs
us down and receive all we truly need in return. Amen.

"I surrender all..."

I first sang these words as a little girl from a hymn in a church with a white-painted steeple. But I have a new perspective when I sing them as a grown-up. I find, to my surprise, that what I'm most reluctant to surrender is *control.*

"I surrender all..."

The words suddenly sound like an invitation to release what I don't really want anyway. Fear, anxiety, striving, perfectionism, trying so very hard. And being, through no fault but my own, alone in these things.

"I surrender all..."

I whisper it under my breath as the song ends, a closing prayer.

I imagine I will come to understand these familiar words in new ways next week, next year, and maybe even when I am silver-haired and ninety-nine, close to my final breath. Because this is the song of our lives as the Jesus people.

"We surrender all..."

And He gives all—everything our weary hearts really need—in return.

Every breath is a reminder that He is near, so today,

just breathe.

–SARAH MAE

You're So Valued

**The LORD values those...
who put their hope in His faithful love.**

PSALM 147:11

*God, our worth comes always and only from You.
We are Your creation, and You alone determine our value.
You say we are worth the life of Your Son—a treasure
beyond what we can even imagine. When insecurity tries
to deceive us, help us remember what's true. Amen.*

A British couple brought a painting to the Antiques Roadshow to find out its value. They didn't particularly like it and had actually moved it to a shed when they redecorated. Imagine their surprise when the painting turned out to be *The Halt in the Desert* by Richard Dadd, a well-known artist. The painting had been missing for a hundred years, and its value (£100,000, or about $150,000 today) set a record on the show.

It didn't matter what the couple thought about the piece; its value came from the one who created it. You and I are works of a master artist as well. Max Lucado says in *Cure for the Common Life*, "Da Vinci painted one *Mona Lisa*. Beethoven composed one Fifth Symphony. And God made one version of you.... We exist to exhibit God, to display His glory. We serve as canvases for His brushstroke, papers for His pen, soil for His seeds, glimpses of His image."

God longs for His children to embrace the worth and value He's given them and then use it to bless others. When we know who we are and whose we are, we're free to love, live with joy, and make a difference in the world.

Coffee for Your Heart

God Is Kind

For You, Lord,
are kind and ready to forgive,
abounding in faithful love to all
who call on You.

PSALM 86:5

God, You speak to us not with condemnation
but with kindness. Yes, You correct us, but not through
criticism—through the life-giving, affirming conviction of
Your Holy Spirit. When we hear a harsh voice
in our minds, help us to remember it's not You
and listen instead to what's true. Amen.

How can we know and hear God's voice? I sat a table full of women one evening talking about this very topic. Someone said, "God's voice is always kind, so if what I'm hearing in my mind isn't kind, then it's not from God."

When I woke up the next morning, I was still thinking about this statement. It seemed so obvious, but I'd not thought of it quite that way before. I reflected on the internal accusations and expectations I sometimes hear.

Those mandates might push me to be outwardly compliant, but the tone is always one of harshness and criticism. When I hear such things, I feel guilt and shame. There is nothing motivating, reassuring, comforting, encouraging, or helpful about criticism and condemnation.

Once we recognize what we're tuned into isn't from God, we can ask Him to help us embrace the truth instead. We can hear His voice through His Word, through the safe people in our lives, and through learning to listen in the quiet moments.

God is speaking to us in a thousand different ways. Every single one comes down to the same message, the one we most long to hear: *you are loved.*

You Have *Amazing* Grace

God is able to make every grace
overflow to you, so that in every way,
always having everything you need,
you may excel in every good work.

II CORINTHIANS 9:8

*God, we need Your grace every moment, every day, in
every way. Your grace not only saves us, it also sustains
us. It is for eternity, but it's also for right here, right now,
too. Help us remember Your grace will never run out, and
every time we need more, we can run to You. Amen.*

"Amazing grace, how sweet the sound that saved a wretch like me."

Every single morning we wake up with a vision of who we want to be and what we want to do. Every single night we fall asleep knowing we didn't completely fulfill that vision. *And that's okay.*

God already knew that would be true the moment we opened our eyes. He knows it will be true tomorrow and every day until we're home with Him and His work in us is complete.

What can trip us up, wear us out, and leave us discouraged is not acknowledging that reality. It's when we say, "Jesus saved me by His grace, but the rest is up to me."

No, Jesus saved us by His grace and He'll sustain us with it in every breath, every heartache, every failure. Grace is not a one-time event—it is an ongoing experience. It is with us every step of our broken, beautiful journey.

"Through many dangers, toils, and snares,
I have already come;
'Tis grace hath brought me safe thus far,
And grace will lead me home."

My life
will never be
mistake-free.

But one thing
I do know is that
it will all be
full of God's grace.

–JENNIFER UECKERT

 God Will Encourage You

**May our Lord Jesus Christ himself
and God our Father, who has loved us and
given us eternal encouragement and good hope
by grace, encourage your hearts and
strengthen you in every good work and word.**
II THESSALONIANS 2:16–17

*God, You are our Encourager. Thank You
that when life lets us down, You lift us up.
When we feel empty, You fill us. When we're disappointed,
You give us hope. Pour out Your encouragement to us
and through us today. Amen.*

The word *encouragement* appears far more times in the New Testament than the Old. Encouragement is described as coming from two sources—God and each other. And unlike simple compliments or kind words, encouragement is rooted in truth. It brings us back to what's realer than real. It reminds our hearts that what we see or experience right now is not the full story. There is more to life and more to us than meets the eye.

Encouragement literally means to help give someone courage. It helps us get back up, face our day with joy, and fulfill the purpose God has for us. It's more than a simple pat on the back or a feel-good pep talk. It's fuel for our faith that provides what we need to move forward even on the most difficult of days.

You are an encourager, called by God and commissioned to strengthen the hearts of people. You have all you need to make a difference in the lives of whoever you meet today.

The Encouragement Project

You Can *Slow* Down

I remember the days of old;
I meditate on all You have done;
I reflect on the work of Your hands.

PSALM 143:5

*God, our lives and minds tend to be full and move fast.
But You offer us the opportunity to slow down, to
remember who You are, to think of all You've done for us,
and to reflect on what's really true. Right now we pause
and turn our thoughts and hearts to You. Amen.*

What if the words of the psalmist—*remember, meditate, reflect*—offer us a three-step process, a way of slowing ourselves down and connecting with God?

To remember means to recount or be mindful. It can be easy to overlook what has come before. Moses told the Israelites over and over, "Remember...." We can do the same by asking this simple question: What has God brought me through?

"Meditate" simply means to think about something in an intentional way. In other words, we're not just recalling specific events but considering who's behind them. We can ask ourselves, "Where can I see God's hand in my life?"

Once we recognize God's hand in our lives, we can reflect on what He has done for us. This leads to gratitude, praise, and growth. We can ask, "What am I grateful for today and what have I learned that will help me grow tomorrow?"

We live in a world that tells us we must always keep moving. But sometimes what we need most is to pause for a few moments so that we can remember, meditate, and reflect.

Yes,
Jesus Loves You

You will know the truth,
and the truth will set you free.

JOHN 8:32

God, there are so many voices trying to get our attention.
Sometimes the lies we hear can get so loud. Yet You are
always whispering to us, calling to us, and speaking to us
with love. We choose truth. We choose Your Word.
We choose to believe what You say today. Amen.

I wake not to the sound of the alarm clock but to the lies ringing in my ears....

You're not good enough.

You don't have what it takes.

You're going to let people down.

I get up and head outside for a walk. As I do so, one simple phrase comes to mind, *"Jesus loves me, this I know."* I can't think of anything else. It's all I have, all I know for sure. I start emphasizing a different word with each step....

JESUS loves me, this I know.

Jesus LOVES me, this I know.

Jesus loves ME, this I know.

The world might tell me that I need more self-esteem to defeat those lies, to calm my racing heart. But what I need, most of all, is to simply remember that I have a Savior. That I always have been and always will be loved just as I am.

Sometimes I think I need to know everything. But I'm finding, more often than not, what I really need is to remember one thing...

Jesus loves me, this I know.

God designed us
for relationship—

*with Him
and with others.*

—KATHY HOWARD

Discomfort Won't Defeat You

We are afflicted in every way but not crushed;
we are perplexed but not in despair;
we are persecuted but not abandoned;
we are struck down but not destroyed.

II CORINTHIANS 4:8–9

God, we are creatures who love comfort. You understand this, and yet You sometimes call us out of our comfort zones to places we never thought we would go. When that happens, strengthen our faith, guide our steps, and help us to persevere in Your plan. Amen.

Dr. Stuart Brown, an expert on the subject of play, shares that even in the most enjoyable experiences of our lives, there is always a bit of discomfort.

He describes what a friend learned about this on a diving trip: "The boat ride out was jarring as the boat slammed through a choppy sea, and the sky looked stormy. My friend was griping about all these things.... Finally, the guide said, 'You know, Josh, you are never going to have peak experiences if you don't let yourself go through some discomfort.'"

When we limit change or even enjoyment in our lives to the times when everything falls into place just as we want, it's a bit like refusing to drive unless every stoplight we come across is green. There will always be discomfort to push through, setbacks to endure, mistakes to overcome. Yet when we look back, we often see that those were the most meaningful parts of our journey. That resistance along the way shapes who we are in ways we often don't expect, and we're stronger for it in the end.

Life is never normal. Timing is never perfect. Conditions are never really right. If you know this is something God wants you to do, move forward anyway.

The "Do What You Can" Plan

God *Understands* It All

Trust in the LORD with all your heart,
and do not rely on your own understanding;
in all your ways know Him,
and He will make your paths straight.

PROVERBS 3:5–6

*God, You know everything about our past, present,
and future. Nothing that happens in our lives is
a surprise to You. When we try to understand it all,
help our hearts remember we don't have to
because we can trust You. Amen.*

It's the "do not rely on your own understanding" part in Proverbs chapter 3 that's hard for me. When I don't know where I'm headed in the next moment or day or year, I feel stressed and anxious. I can assume I have to guess or just do my best rather than relying on something outside myself, like the GPS in my car or the Spirit of God within me.

I'm in a season that feels confusing and uncertain. Just this morning a friend said to me, "Maybe you're not supposed to figure this out." My whole soul sighed in relief at those words.

So just in case you're wired a bit like me (or love someone who is) let's tell ourselves all over again: *We don't have to figure out everything on our own.*

Yes, not relying on our own understanding may feel awkward and as if we're losing control. But I'm slowly discovering that letting go of control is actually what I want and need most. Trust, not trying hard, is what leads me into peace and rest and even joy. It's the only way home for my wandering, worrying heart.

Purpose
Beats Productivity

I call to God Most High,
to God who fulfills His purpose for me.

PSALM 57:2

God, You spoke the world into being, split the Red Sea,
and called the stars into the night sky. You will never have
a problem with productivity, and it's not what You want
most from us. Give us the courage and discernment to
choose purposeful living over producing today. Amen.

The laundry is still unfolded, the emails unanswered, the to-do list undone. I sigh and ask, "Have I been productive at all today?" In that quiet moment, it seems my heart hears a reassuring reminder: *Life isn't about being productive. It's about being purposeful.*

I've often believed the lie that God's first priority is what I can produce: a basket of neatly folded laundry, a dozen email responses, a to-do list with check marks. But the truth is, there are other things that matter just as much or more. Just because something doesn't have tangible results doesn't mean it doesn't have eternal impact.

I'm no longer going to ask myself, "Have I been productive today?" Instead I'm going to ask, "Have I been purposeful?" To me that simply means *living in love*. Sometimes love looks like laundry and answering email and checking off what's on my list. But sometimes it looks like the exact opposite, like we've done "nothing" at all. And that's okay too.

Our works will never be what determines our true worth.

*My significance and worth
as a human being was settled
a long time ago*

on the cross.

—MICHELLE S. LAZUREK

Your Head Is *Held High*

You, LORD, are a shield around me, my glory,
and the one who lifts up my head.

PSALM 3:3

*God, You are the One who lifts our heads,
and this is the beautiful thing: when You lift our heads
it is an invitation to look at You, to remember
who we are and Whose we are. We turn our eyes
and our hearts toward You today. Amen.*

Whether you're at the end of a hard day, in the middle of celebrating, or somewhere in between, there's some truth you need to hear and it's this: you are not your circumstances.

In all the moments of your life, you are a woman of grace and strength. Even when you feel weak, you have divine power within you that is able to get you through anything. And you are loved far more than you can even imagine.

How you feel today, what you're facing, even what others may say doesn't change that—and never can. Who you are is secure forever. And you are a daughter of God, a holy princess, a woman who is chosen and cherished. Nothing and no one can take that away from you.

You have within you a God who is bigger than your bad days and stronger than your circumstances, and He will never let you go. He has promised that nothing will defeat you and no one can stand against you.

So keep pressing forward. Hold your head up high and know that you are loved. Yesterday. Today. Tomorrow.

If We Could Have Coffee...

You Have a Calling

God is faithful;
you were called by Him into fellowship
with His Son, Jesus Christ our Lord.

I CORINTHIANS 1:9

God, we can get so fixated on what "our calling" might be,
but what we can know each and every day is that
You call us to yourself. Help us to remember
what You want most is not our hands but our hearts,
not our efforts but our devotion, not what we can do,
but the love we have for You. Amen.

When we ask, "Is God calling me?" the answer is always, "Absolutely." He's calling each and every one of us *to Himself*. That's the calling we all share.

Within that calling there will be things He asks us to do, steps of obedience He wants us to take. Whatever those are, we will never feel fully ready to do them. *That is a good thing.* Because it's not about us. It's about Him. Our brokenness, our weaknesses, and our failures are not enough to stop our unstoppable God.

I am living proof of that truth. I imagine you are too.

That's why we need each other. As my friend and fellow writer Jennifer Watson says, "You don't have to show up perfect; you just have to show up. You are needed.... We are not meant to walk through life alone. Freedom is something we live together, not just on our own." Needing other people isn't weakness; it's wisdom. It's the design God has always had in mind.

So let's not give in to the fear or insecurity. Let's answer God's call. Let's draw closer to each other and to Him today.

Courage *Can't Be Stopped*

Be strong, and let your heart be courageous,
all you who put your hope in the LORD.

PSALM 31:24

*God, thank You that we don't have to stay where we are
until we are unafraid. Instead, we can take one trembling
step at a time, trusting that You will give us what we need
to do so. You will make us stronger as we go. You will get
us to where You want us to be. We can trust You. Amen.*

Fear is inevitable, but letting it stop us is optional. It may try to tell us we're too weak to do God's will. It may taunt us and say we're not ready or someone else could do it better. But we don't have to listen to its voice. We don't have to give in to its lies.

If we wait until we don't ever feel fear about doing God's will, then we will never obey. He's okay with our trembling hands, knocking knees, and pounding hearts. After all, He designed the bodies that cause them—and He spent thirty-three years in one.

When we experience anxiety or fear, the enemy can try to use it as an opportunity to make us feel guilt or shame. That's when we can pause and ask God for help, knowing He understands and never condemns us.

God will come alongside us in our uncertain moments and give us the reassurance we need. Then He'll lead us out of fear and into courage.

We can
trust God's plan
in our lives

even when
we have no idea
what our future
may hold.

—SHELLY WILDMAN

You're *Braver* than You Know

I have told you these things so that in Me you may
have peace. You will have suffering in this world.
Be courageous! I have conquered the world.

JOHN 16:33

*God, You are the One who makes us braver than
we ever could be on our own. You are the One
who empowers us to do more than we ever thought
we could. Even when our emotions tell us to run away,
You help us stay and stand strong. Amen.*

I can't think of a single time "brave" showed up as an emotion in my world. I know what it is to *be* brave. But in those times, often what I still feel is fear. The pounding of my heart and the quickening of my breath. The spinning of the earth beneath my feet and the sense that I may be full-out crazy to go through with what I'm about to do.

And as I think about this, I realize maybe I've misunderstood what "brave" feels like: I thought it was a roar and a lunge. But maybe it is a whisper and a trembling step. I thought it was loud and bold. Perhaps it is quiet and almost invisible. I imagined it would mean the absence of all insecurity. Yet I'm wondering now if it's faith dancing the two-step with doubt.

If this is so, then what makes me act bravely is also what scares me silly.

This lets me breathe a sigh of relief. Because it means I don't have to wait to be filled with confidence and courage before I can do anything—I can just show up anyway. If that's so, then I have more courage than I thought. And more answers than I realized. And so do you.

Strong, Brave, Loved

You're a World Changer

According to the grace given to us,
we have different gifts.

ROMANS 12:6

God, You are the only One who does truly big things.
You are also the One who makes even the small things
in our lives sacred. Help us to use the gifts You've entrusted
to us wherever we are for the benefit of whoever
You place in front of us today. Amen.

Someone recently asked me whether I considered myself to be a world changer. When I got my wits about me again, I said this: "My sweet Daddy once told me, 'I pray every day that your words will touch the heart of one woman who will touch the hearts of her family who will touch the hearts of their community who will touch the world.' "

I believe being a world changer simply means touching the heart of one person at a time through whatever gifts we've been given right where we are today. That one person for you might be a friend, a coworker, someone in your family, or a stranger on the street. Your gift might be words or encouraging, organizing or baking, leading or creating spreadsheets.

Let's never believe the myth I'm sometimes tempted to, the one that says only certain people get to be world changers, the kind who seem to do big, extraordinary things. *God alone is big and extraordinary.* He uses small, ordinary people to change the world every day because that's the only kind there are, the only kind there will ever be.

That includes you and me.

You're Needed Now

For the LORD is good,
and His faithful love endures forever;
His faithfulness, through all generations.

PSALM 100:5

*God, You are the Lord of yesterday, today, and forever.
You are the God of every generation that has been and
each one that is yet to be. You are the One writing history
and our story. You have placed us here for such a time
as this, and we want to glorify You. Amen.*

To the senior sisters: you are needed, and it's never too late for God to use you. Please know we long for your presence and hard-won wisdom. It's so much harder to walk well without someone going before us.

To those of us in middle age: let's not miss the divine hidden among the mundane and ordinary. We can touch a life whether we're holding a microphone or warming up mac and cheese in the microwave. What's visible isn't more valuable.

To those younger: it's never too early for God to use you either. Don't wait to feel ready. We need your optimism and energy, your fresh perspective, and your daring personality. If you received something yesterday—even five minutes ago—then you have something to give to someone else.

Together we can look back with gratefulness for what God has done and look forward with anticipation for what He has yet to do. And we can each choose to make a difference where we are now. We all have something to offer. We all have something to receive. We are better together.

God doesn't
just work
despite me—

He works
through me.

—SARAH J. HAUSER

You Can Embrace Rest

**But those who trust in the LORD
will renew their strength;
they will soar on wings like eagles;
they will run and not become weary,
they will walk and not faint.**

ISAIAH 40:31

*God, from the very beginning of the world, You have
designed rest to be part of our lives. And even when
we're busy on the outside, You can give us rest
on the inside. When we start to strive and push,
draw us back into trust and peace. Amen.*

Rest, not hustle, has always been and will always be God's desire and design for us.

In our culture, we define rest narrowly. We see it as simply stopping our work. But to God it is so much more. Rest is a state of peace and security. Yes, sometimes it is an actual, tangible pause, but it is also a way of living differently no matter what we're doing.

I have stared at the ceiling in the night, completely still, and not been at all tranquil as worries shook my mind. I have been in the middle of giving a speech to thousands and felt absolutely at peace inside even though my lips and schedule and words seemed to be moving at warp speed.

Yes, our bodies need regular rest, but I think that is only the first layer, the very surface of what God wants for us. Rest is not simply the lack of activity, but the presence of trust. Because trust is a kind of inner leaning, an intentional reliance on someone else.

We can live in rest because we live in God's love always, from our quietest moments to our busiest days.

Hope Your Heart Needs

God Is Your
Hiding Place

For You are my hiding place;
You protect me from trouble.
You surround me with songs of victory.

PSALM 32:7 NLT

*God, we can always go to You and trust that You will be
a safe place for our hurts and our hearts, our victories
and stumbles, our dreams and deepest desires.
You are our ultimate security and we trust You
with everything we are, with all we have. Amen.*

When we're afraid, our natural tendency is to hide. We physically or emotionally retreat to where it feels safer. I've done this by literally diving under the covers in my bedroom. Or I've hidden my heart by putting on a smiling face when I felt broken inside.

God knows this tendency we have as humans, and He doesn't tell us *not* to hide. We aren't in trouble for this instinct. What God does want to change is *where* and *how* we hide. God Himself wants to be our "hiding place."

A hiding place is a shelter. It's a space of security. It's a location where we feel loved. When God says He is our hiding place, it means we are always welcome in His presence. "Open door, open heart" is one of my grandma's favorite sayings. It seems God extends a similar offer to us.

Whatever we're facing, we can come to God with it. He is our strength and security. He gives us courage and makes us brave. His love and truth are bigger and stronger than anything we fear.

You've Been Renamed

When Jesus saw him, He said,
"You are Simon, son of John.
You will be called Cephas"
(which is translated "Peter").

JOHN 1:42

God, You know us even better than we know ourselves.
You see our potential when we see our problems.
You see our strengths when we only see our struggles.
You see beyond our humanity to who You've made us
for eternity. Align our perspective
with Yours today. Amen.

Jesus gave Simon not just a new name, but a new identity. "Cephas" or "Peter" both mean "rock."

I wonder if Peter had ever thought of himself as a rock. Over the next few chapters in Scripture, he shows himself to be volatile, unsteady, impulsive. But Jesus calls out something in Peter and he grows into it, becomes it. Jesus does the same in us.

How would you define yourself today? Mama, wife, friend, sister, coworker. Introvert, extrovert. Southern, Northern, Australian. Or maybe the words are not so kind: failure, addict, broken, insecure, unworthy. Whatever the description might be, Jesus has more to add: beloved, chosen, accepted, forgiven, free, more than a conqueror.

Like Peter, it's okay if we can't feel, see, or even fully understand what God says is true of us yet. What matters is that we don't trust our human identity to be our ultimate destiny. So when the world around us tries to tell us who we are, let's pause and listen for the only voice that gets the final say.

God takes broken things
and makes them

beautiful.

–BECKY L. MCCOY

You're Here for a Purpose

**The LORD will fulfill His purpose for me.
LORD, Your faithful love endures forever...**

PSALM 138:8

*God, we live in a world full of choices
and opportunities. We're so grateful for that,
and yet we also need wisdom to choose what's truly best.
Guide us into the plans You have for us and show us
which way to go with each step. Amen.*

My college mentor leans back and says words that will stay with me for decades to come: "Holley, the hardest choices in life aren't between bad and good. They're between good and best."

Becoming a thriving adult requires discovering our limits and then figuring out a filter that helps us choose what truly matters most. In today's world, there will always be plenty of choices. But not everything we can do is something we *should* do. Even if someone else really, really wants us to do it. God created us for a specific purpose, and He has a divine plan that can be accomplished through us.

You are here for a reason, and you are irreplaceable. God wants you to take ownership of your life. He wants you to live proactively rather than reactively. There will always be someone who's willing to tell you who you should be and what you should do. But God doesn't want you to be like anyone but Jesus—and only He knows how your one wild and precious life is best spent.

You're Already Amazing LifeGrowth Guide

You Can Have
True Success

Commit your actions to the LORD,
and your plans will succeed.
PROVERBS 16:3 NLT

God, we'd like to know how everything in our lives
will go. But that's impossible. It's comforting to know
that You don't measure success like we do.
You see success as obedience rather than results.
Give us the courage to commit all we do to You,
trusting You to make it a true success. Amen.

I'm doing a final review of a project when an unexpected wave of fear sweeps over me. I suddenly remember the work I have completed in the quiet will soon be seen by a crowd.

I'm not alone in that feeling. The accountant who must present her spreadsheets in a meeting knows it. The mom whose child is launching into the world understands it. The runner who trains on the back roads and then takes her place at the starting line battles it.

I began to ask, "How can I make sure this goes well?" And a verse from Proverbs popped into my mind: "Commit your actions to the LORD, and your plans will succeed" (Proverbs 16:3 NLT). I paused and considered the words. Was this a guarantee from God that everything would go the way I'd like? Life experience and the rest of His Word would seem to tell me otherwise.

Slowly I began to see the true meaning: success isn't about outcome; it's about obedience.

The "success" this verse talks about is set in motion not when the results are in but as soon as we say, "God, I give this to You." He thinks differently than we do. To Him, every obedient "yes" is already a success.

There's No Stopping You

I will praise You
because I have been remarkably
and wondrously made.

PSALM 139:14

God, You are the One who makes us who we are.
We are Your creations. When we're tempted to focus
on our flaws and imperfections, help us instead to praise
You. No matter how we feel or what anyone may have
told us, we are not mistakes. We are miracles
made in Your image. Amen.

Pssst . . . pull up a chair and I'll tell you a secret. You'd better lean in close for this one. Ready? You don't have to do more, be more, have more. I'm sure there are security alarms going off somewhere. You should probably hide this book when your in-laws come over. And this could be the makings of a Sunday-morning scandal. But it's true.

It's the kind of true that will change your life, set you free, and make you wake up smiling for the first time in a long time. I know because that's what it did for me (and believe me, for this non-morning girl that's nothing short of miraculous).

Even if we've never met, I know this about you: you're a daughter of God, a holy princess, a woman created with strengths you've yet to fully grasp, and a story that's still being written by the divine Author himself. And if you really take hold of who you are and what you're called to do, there will be no stopping you. That's because there's no stopping Him in you—and He's got bigger plans for your life than you've even imagined.

You're Already Amazing

You are
a daughter
of the King,

and your story is significant.

—LISA-JO BAKER

You're *Not Quitting*

**May the Lord direct your hearts
to God's love and Christ's endurance.**

II THESSALONIANS 3:5

*God, sometimes it seems easier to give up than to keep
moving forward. When we feel weary, be our strength.
When we want to stop, help us take one more step. When
we're tempted to quit, give us what we need to carry on.
We will persevere with You. Amen.*

God loves messy people. The wild ones. The kind we might pass by. David the murderer and adulterer. Peter the fisherman with rough edges. Rahab the lady of the night who found the light.

It doesn't make any sense to us. We would pick the ones who have it all together. The ones who didn't cause such a scene. The ones who played by the rules.

So what do the people God chooses have in common? They don't quit. The mistakes they make are astounding. The baggage they carry could fill a huge truck. The stunts they pull would get most of us fired. But they never stop. They fall down and get back up. They say the wrong thing and then repent. They fail and stubbornly press forward anyway.

I imagine you're the same way. You never quit pursuing Jesus. You never quit saying yes when He asks you to do something crazy. You never quit letting Him teach you through your mistakes. You never quit giving it one more try, even when you're scared silly.

That is what brings God joy. Not when you're "perfect" on the outside. Not when you have a tidy existence. Not when you get it right the first time. Nope, God loves it when you will stop at nothing to have more of Him in your life.

Opening the Door to Your God-Sized Dream

Help Is on the Way

Therefore, we may boldly say,
The Lord is my helper;
I will not be afraid.
What can man do to me?

HEBREWS 13:6

God, You are the Helper who is always with us,
always for us, always working on our behalf.
We pray that we would reflect Your heart
by helping others too. Show us our
divine assignments today. Amen.

In the documentary *Won't You Be My Neighbor?* beloved television personality Mr. Rogers says, "When I was a boy and I would see scary things in the news, my mother would say to me, 'Look for the helpers. You will always find people who are helping.'" The film makes it clear he not only looked for the helpers, but chose to become one.

We all have our own way of helping. Maybe you teach, lead, raise children, or make beautiful art. Maybe you're walking with someone you love through a hard season so they won't be alone in it. Maybe you pray in the quiet when no one is watching. This is all helping. Never underestimate the worth of it.

And the reassuring truth we all need is that God is a helper too—and more than that, He is *our* helper. On the days when we become a bit tired, when it all seems like too much, He says to us, "I will strengthen you and help you" (Isaiah 41:10 NLT). Fred Rogers, an ordained minister, knew this to be true.

Let's keep looking for the helpers. Let's keep *being* the helpers too.

You're Being Faithful

**Whoever is faithful in very little
is also faithful in much.**

LUKE 16:10

*God, when life is challenging, we want safety and control
and to hold on to what's familiar. But what we truly need
is to just take the next step of faith with You. We discover
what we need along the way because You will provide it.
We're listening, we're receiving, we're obeying. Amen.*

Imagine the scene: Jesus has been crucified. The disciples' lives are in turmoil. They're unsure of what the future holds. Peter wants something familiar: "I'm going fishing" (John 21:3).

Then Jesus appears, although they don't yet know it's Him, and He tells them to let out their nets one more time. They catch so many fish they can hardly handle them all.

This is faithfulness. It's continuing to cast the net because Jesus says so. Even when we've been up all night. Even when we're weary. Even when we're confused. Even when we're discouraged and want to quit.

If you're putting pressure on yourself today to do more, be more, or achieve more, then pause and take a deep breath. *Just be faithful.*

If you're comparing yourself to others in life or ministry and feel you're falling short, refocus on your own journey. *Just be faithful.*

If you're striving for perfection and trying to make everyone happy, let go of those unrealistic expectations. *Just be faithful.*

Just do what you can, where you are, with what you have, to love God and others today. Then do it again one more time.

God is with us
in our waiting,
working all things for

our good and
His glory.

—KAITLYN BOUCHILLON

Jesus Is the Answer

For every one of God's promises is "Yes" in Him.
Therefore, through Him we also say
"Amen" to the glory of God.

II CORINTHIANS 1:20

God, You are the One who hears our prayers,
who sees the desires of our hearts. We come to You
with our questions and requests, our struggles and
uncertainty, knowing You may not give us
answers but You will always be the one
answer we truly need. Amen.

"Amen" means "so be it." It is a forceful word, a call to action, a powerful alliance between us and heaven's will. "Amen" is also a name of Jesus (Revelation 3:14). So when we say this word, we are actually calling on Him.

When we ask God for a Savior, Jesus in the manger is the amen.

When we beg for forgiveness, Jesus on the cross is the amen.

When we need new life and hope, Jesus exiting the empty tomb is the amen.

When we long for comfort, peace, joy, and all that belongs to us as believers, Jesus in our everyday lives is the amen and amen and amen.

This doesn't mean we will automatically get what we want just by invoking this word. It is both a frustration and a relief to realize that "amen" is not "so do it" but "so be it." Because this means, ultimately, when we say amen, we are praying for God's best and yielding to His will.

This is what I know now, what I'll know forever: "Amen" is more than where a prayer ends. It's where every answer begins—always and only with Jesus.

Hope Your Heart Needs

You're on a *Mission*

Jesus said to them again,
"Peace be with you.
As the Father has sent Me,
I also send you."

JOHN 20:21

*God, You have a mission for each of us,
and it's to share Your love, to speak Your truth,
and to do Your will. Thank You that we don't have to get on
a plane or go far away to live that out. We can do so
wherever You've placed us today. Amen.*

"Missionary" simply means someone who has or is on a mission. In that case, we all bear that name.

Yes, let's give special care and honor to those for whom it is also an occupation. But let's not forget—we also have been sent. We were sent the second that first spark of life flickered in our mother's womb. To this earth. And now to wherever we are today.

So let's take off our shoes and our misconceptions and declare that this is holy ground. Because God is here. He is in this moment. Perhaps even more miraculous, He is in us. And that is what He wants us to bring to wherever we are, wherever we go—not our talent or our goodness, our knowledge or our niceness. *God Himself.*

Do you want to know where God is asking you to serve and bless and bring Him glory right now? You only need to look down at the one foot of humble, sacred earth beneath your feet. The only place on this spinning globe where both you and God are present in this moment.

You're *Healing* as You Go

Ten men with leprosy met Him.
They stood at a distance and raised their voices,
saying, "Jesus, Master, have mercy on us!"
When He saw them, He told them,
"Go and show yourselves to the priests."
And while they were going, they were cleansed.

LUKE 17:12–14

God, thank You that I don't have to be perfect to be part
of Your plan. You aren't asking me to hold back until my
healing is complete. Instead, You invite me to obey today.
You give me a path to follow. You are transforming
my life with every step. Amen.

I think of the story of the ten lepers. "Jesus, Master, have mercy on us!" they cried. His answer? "Go show yourselves to the priests."

It's what happens next that amazes me. "And as they went, they were cleansed" (NIV). It's tempting to hold back and stay stuck because we think we have to be completely healed before we *go and show*. We want our story to already have the happy ending, the bow to be tied around the package, the scars to be faded into invisibility. But I've found, as the lepers did, that the healing often happens along the way.

You don't have to wait for your healing to be complete before you start moving forward. You don't have to be whole before God sends you out. Of course we want healing to be a one-time, instantaneous event. We can even feel guilty if it's not. But I've found healing is more often a process. Sometimes when we ask God to move, He's asking us the same.

Nothing has the power to hold you back.

You are already worthy.

And God is already at work.

*God is the creator
of new beginnings,
and He desires
to come alongside us*

*with a
fresh start.*

—JEN SCHMIDT

You're Going to *Finish*

**I have fought the good fight,
I have finished the race,
I have kept the faith.**

II TIMOTHY 4:7

*God, when we walk with You, it's not about going fast;
it's about going far. It's about serving You faithfully
for a lifetime. When we're tempted to sprint, remind us
to slow down and stay close. You are cheering us on
with every step, and we're so grateful. Amen.*

If you plan to do something not for a while but for as long as you can because you love it, feel called to it, and the touch of heaven is on it, then sprinting is not the solution. Faith, as Eugene Peterson says, is about "a long obedience in the same direction."

This makes no sense in our instant world. It's upside down in the time of social media updates. It seems less sexy and exciting than the fast and the fancy. But it's reassuring too, isn't it? To know we don't have to push so hard. We don't have to "go big or go home." We can just be obedient and leave the results to God.

I hope sometimes we get to go fast. That there are moments with the wind in our hair, the heart in our chest pumping wildly, and the ground a blur beneath our feet. But I'm asking Jesus even more that we go far. That we make it around all the bends in the road. Or watch the leaves turn from green to amber gold. Have like-hearted companions with us. Take the next step, then the next step, all the way. Let's keep running our race at our pace. We're doing better than we know.

See you at the finish.

Fiercehearted

You're Cheered On

We have come to know and
to believe the love that God has for us.

I JOHN 4:16

*God, You have brought us so far, and You promise that
You will continue to be with us every step of the way.
Thank You that we are never alone and always loved.
Our lives are in Your hands, and You will carry out
Your purpose and plans for us. Amen.*

Pause for a moment and think back on how far you've already come. Remember the obstacles you once thought would block your way. Think of the times you wanted to quit and how you took one more step. Picture the battles where you were knocked down and got back up again.

Those are not small things. They are significant victories. They are reasons to celebrate. And what God has already done in your life, He will continue to do.

God will continue to make you an overcomer.

He will continue to help you persevere.

He will continue to take you by the hand and pick you up every single time.

There is nothing that can defeat you. There is no one who can stand against you when God is on your side. There will never be a situation or a circumstance that can take you out of God's hands. You have hope and a future.

God will continue to work out His plans for you. He will always love you. He will always be *for* you, forever cheering you on.

Acknowledgments

Special thanks to Revell, a division of Baker Publishing Group, for permission to include content adapted from Holley Gerth's books in Cheering You On. To find all of Holley's books, visit your favorite book retailer, dayspring.com, or holleygerth.com.

Endnotes

There's So Much Ahead for You: Gerth, Holley. *Strong, Brave, Loved* (E-book Shorts): *21 Ways to a Fiercehearted Life*. Grand Rapids: Revell, 2018. Kindle.

God Will Come Through for You: Gerth, Holley. *You're Already Amazing: Embracing Who You Are, Becoming All God Created You to Be*. Grand Rapids: Revell, 2012. Kindle. Quote Priscilla Shirer. *One in a Million: Journey to Your Promised Land*. Nashville: B&H Publishing Group, 2010.

Most People Don't, but You Do: Gerth, Holley. *You're Already Amazing: Embracing Who You Are, Becoming All God Created You to Be*. Grand Rapids: Revell, 2012. Kindle.

God Is Your Source: Gerth, Holley. *You're Made for a God-Sized Dream: Opening the Door to All God Has for You*. Grand Rapids: Revell, 2013. Kindle.

Praise Is Powerful: Gerth, Holley. *What Your Heart Needs for the Hard Days: 52 Encouraging Truths to Hold On To*. Grand Rapids: Revell, 2014. Kindle.

God Will Guide You: Gerth, Holley. *You're Going to Be Okay: Encouraging Truth Your Heart Needs to Hear, Especially on the Hard Days*. Grand Rapids: Revell, 2014. Kindle.

Your Brokenness Is Beautiful: Gerth, Holley. *You're Loved No Matter What: Freeing Your Heart from the Need to Be Perfect*. Grand Rapids: Revell, 2015. Kindle.

You're So Valued: Gerth, Holley. *Coffee for Your Heart: 40 Morning of Life-Changing Encouragement*. Eugene: Harvest House, 2017. Kindle. Quote by Max Lucado. *Cure for the Common Life: Living in Your Sweet Spot*. Nashville: Thomas Nelson, 2011. Kindle.

God Will Encourage You: Gerth, Holley. *The Encouragement Project* (E-book Shorts): *21 Heart-to-Heart Ways to Show You Care*. Grand Rapids: Revell, 2015. Kindle

Discomfort Won't Defeat You: Gerth, Holley. *The "Do What You Can" Plan* (E-book Shorts): *21 Days to Make Any Area of Your Life Better.* Grand Rapids: Revell, 2013. Kindle. Quote by Stuart Brown, M.D. *Play: How it Shapes the Brain, Opens the Imagination, and Invigorates the Soul* (p.202).New York City: Avery, 2009. Kindle.

Your Head Is Held High: Gerth, Holley. *If We Could Have Coffee...* (E-book Shorts): *30 Days of Heart-to-Heart Encouragement.* Grand Rapids: Revell, 2014. Kindle.

You Have a Calling: Watson, Jennifer. *Freedom! The Gutsy Pursuit of Breakthrough and the Life Beyond It,* 196–197. Bloomington: Bethany House Publishers, 2019.

You're Braver than You Know: Gerth, Holley. *Strong, Brave, Loved* (E-book Shorts): *21 Ways to a Fiercehearted Life.* Grand Rapids: Revell, 2018. Kindle.

You Can Embrace Rest: Gerth, Holley. *Hope Your Heart Needs: 52 Encouraging Reminders of How God Cares for You.* Grand Rapids. Revell, 2018. Kindle.

You're Here for a Purpose: Gerth, Holley. *You're Already Amazing LifeGrowth Guide: Embracing Who You Are, Becoming All God Created You to Be.* Grand Rapids. Revell, 2016. Kindle.

There's No Stopping You: *You're Already Amazing: Embracing Who You Are, Becoming All God Created You to Be.* Grand Rapids: Revell, 2012. Kindle.

You're Not Quitting: Gerth, Holley. *Opening the Door to Your God-Sized Dream: 40 Days of Encouragement for Your Heart.* Grand Rapids: Revell, 2013. Kindle.

Help Is on the Way: Rogers, Fred. *Won't You Be My Neighbor?* DVD. Directed by Morgan Neville. Universal City: Focus Features, 2018.

Jesus Is the Answer: Gerth, Holley. *Hope Your Heart Needs: 52 Encouraging Reminders of How God Cares for You.* Grand Rapids. Revell, 2018. Kindle.

You're Going to Finish: Gerth, Holley. *Fiercehearted: Live Fully, Love Bravely.* Grand Rapids. Revell, 2017. Kindle.

LIVE YOUR FAITH

Dear Friend,

This book was prayerfully crafted with you, the reader, in mind—every word, every sentence, every page—was thoughtfully written, designed, and packaged to encourage you...right where you are this very moment. At DaySpring, our vision is to see every person experience the life-changing message of God's love. So, as we worked through rough drafts, design changes, edits and details, we prayed for you to deeply experience His unfailing love, indescribable peace, and pure joy. It is our sincere hope that through these Truth-filled pages your heart will be blessed, knowing that God cares about you—your desires and disappointments, your challenges and dreams.

He knows. He cares. He loves you unconditionally.

BLESSINGS!
THE DAYSPRING BOOK TEAM

Additional copies of this book and
other DaySpring titles can be purchased
at fine retailers everywhere.
Order online at dayspring.com
or
by phone at 1-877-751-4347